I0169139

All the Words Kept Inside

Mary McCormack

Also by Mary McCormack:

Tastes of Sunlight: Haiku for the Seasons (2022)

Copyright © 2023 Mary McCormack
All Rights Reserved.

ISBN-10: 0-9981720-4-0
ISBN-13: 978-0-9981720-4-0

Cover Photo & Design: Mary McCormack

All the Words Kept Inside

All the Words Kept Inside is a haiku journey that starts with divorce and ultimately unfolds into a new beginning. From darkness to light, these selected haiku and micro-poems transform from self-doubt and loneliness into hope and a new mindset. McCormack invites us into her world, where together we are *stepping through cobwebs / into the forest / with a clear mind.* Poems like this one beautifully mark the transition into self-respect and compassion, inspiring readers, too, to emerge from their griefs and look for what gives them joy. This collection reverberates with a voice of empowerment.

—Jacob D. Salzer, author of Unplugged— Haiku & Tanka (Lulu, 2022) and co-author of Returning: Tanka Sequences (Lulu, 2022)

Acknowledgments

Many thanks to all the people who made this book possible – those who offered me a place to stay when I was in a time of need, those who listened to me and made me feel like my words matter, and those who (always) encourage me to write.

releasing a sigh
one more sound
absorbed by the forest

All the Words Kept Inside

the ups and downs
that marriage
didn't last through

when home
isn't home
anymore

what a promise
means
once broken

perspective
shifting into place
tectonic plates

dried snot
on my sweatshirt sleeve
glitters rainbow

in each tear
the words
too hard to say

on my own
the unforgiving world
turns its cheek

falling backward
no one
to catch me

dulled senses
two hours
to eat the oatmeal

overcome
tall grasses bend
with rain

the difference
between having a key
and nothing

hours
disappearing into
anxiety

the tension
of trying to hold in
my emotions

wrestling
my countenance
into a smile

geese lifting off
only so far
the eyes can follow

rainstorm
if i'm gone
what does it matter?

no amount of searching
can bring back
the past

if you just ask
so many secrets
that aren't secrets

what is it
that makes everyone believe
I'm alright?

valerian root tea
the slow drift
off the edge of the world

drowning no hand reaching up to air

you'll get through it
the utter confidence
of everyone else

all alone
a teardrop
touched by sunlight

there but not there loneliness

sleepless night
too many thoughts
to sort into words

some truths
hurt to look upon
for too long

flickering
in and out of shadow
my self-image

opposing forces
and I
got swept under

drowning again
I can't
lift

relaxing my thoughts
into a river
the headache floats away

cradling me
in its words
the fantasy novel

breathe in
beeswax candles
breathe out

darkness in the inkwell words await a quill

crashing through me
all the words
I kept inside

mist forming and reforming my thoughts

writing
to pull myself
up

a blank page
sunlight
blinds my eyes

the overwhelming urge
to lie down in the grass
and sleep forever

so many friends
but no one
to talk to

nowhere
where I'm not
a burden

everyone
has their own life
and sometimes
I'm just
so lonely

talk to me
so I don't have to think
about myself

head tucked
deep into
my own musk

asking for help...
shame runs hot
through my veins

I used to think
pride was foolish
now I'm a fool, too

the difference between
offering and giving
help

fighting back sadness a hug

left with the dishes
Friday night
blues

on my own –
the windows shudder
against the cold

another splash...
will the tears
ever cease?

seeing the light –
no way to get there
but through

black walnuts –
the ground no longer firm
beneath my feet

the arduous path of a tear

sunrise
a tinge of pink
in the white clover

swimming up
out of depression
air

foghorn breaking the stupor

a familiar path
takes me
somewhere new

time
and time again
a crossroads

a spinning leaf
points this way
and that

learning
to love
randomness

sometimes all it takes
is one person asking
what you want

feet wet with dew
sunrise
over the pond

the storm leaves
a single cicada wing
mosaic

finding the way
back
to myself

stepping through cobwebs
into the forest
with a clear mind

waking up
all the sensations
coming back to me

the world
is blooming
again

only when you stop
do you hear them
ripples

tremor
of a monarch's wings
before flight

tangoing
on a beam
of light

wings flapping the sky bursts into song

heartwood
open to the elements

a gentle breeze
opening the door
to my mind

emerge
    emerging…
        emerged

a beam of sunlight
from within
my growing smile

heading out
on my own
dawn's first light

About the Author:

Mary McCormack is a writer and teacher of poetry, fiction, and nonfiction. She was the winner of the 2022 Vancouver Cherry Blossom Haiku Invitational in the US category, and her haiku have been widely published in the US and internationally. She is enchanted by the sun.

Website: www.marymwriter.com

www.ingramcontent.com/pod-product-compliance
Lightning Source LLC
Chambersburg PA
CBHW031615040426
42452CB00006B/539